TOWN & COUNTRY

For Karen Anna

by the same authors
THE YEAR AT MAPLE HILL FARM
A HORSE AND A HOUND
A GOAT AND A GANDER
AN OWL AND THREE PUSSYCATS

Published in the United States in
1985. Crown Publishers, Inc., One Park Avenue, New York, New York 10016
Manufactured in Italy
First published in 1984 in Great Britain by Jonathan Cape Ltd.,
30 Bedford Square, London WCI

Library of Congress Cataloging in Publication Data
Provensen, Alice.
Town and country.
Summary: Describes life in a big city and on a farm near a village.
1. Cities and towns—Juvenile literature.
2. Farms—Juvenile literature. 3. Villages—
Juvenile literature. [1. City and town life.
2. Farm life. 3. Villages] I. Provensen, Martin.
II. Title.
HT119.P76 1984 307 84-12693
ISBN 0-517-55594-8

10 9 8 7 6 5 4 3 2 1
First American Edition

TOWN & COUNTRY

ALICE AND MARTIN PROVENSEN

CROWN PUBLISHERS, INC.
NEW YORK

There are many places to live in the world. You might live in a tent in the desert, or in a bamboo hut on a South seas island. You could even live in an igloo on an iceberg. But most people who live in the Western world live in a town or in a house in the country.

They might live in a hamlet, which is smaller than a village, or a village which is smaller than a town, or a town which is smaller than a city, or a city, which is BIG. These tracks lead to a big city somewhere in the world.

In a big city, you may live in a furnished
room or a town house or a mansion,
but most people who live in a really big city
live in an apartment and
almost everyone who visits a big city
stays at a hotel.

If you have a room at the top
and a window with a view,
you can see so many things.

You can see planes flying overhead
and pigeons on the windowsills.

You can see ships at the dock
and boats on the river.

There are office buildings
and factory buildings
and clock towers and water towers
and cathedral steeples to see.

When you look down
you look down on hundreds of cars
and hundreds and thousands
of people in the streets.

They seem as small as toys and as busy as ants
when you look down on them
from really high up.

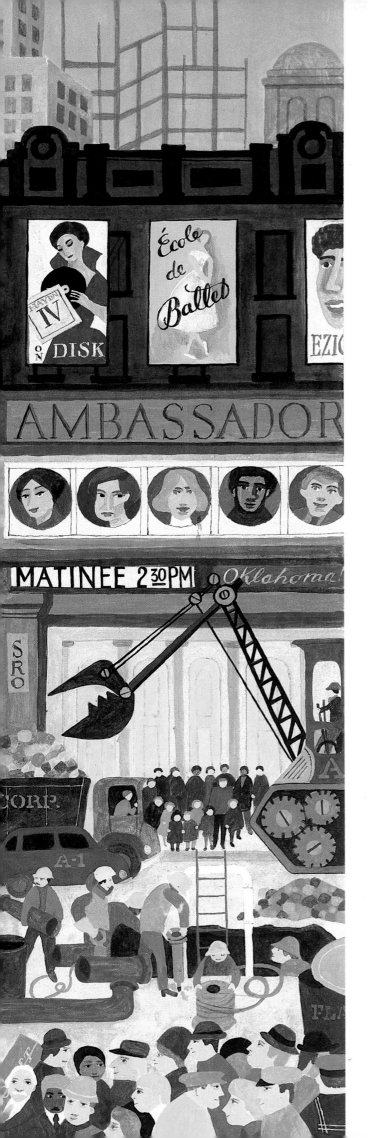

There is always something worth looking at
and listening to on the streets of a big city.
There are all those busy people! White people,
black people, tan people, big and little people, fat
and thin people, coming and going,
walking fast, always in a hurry. You don't know
their names but they look interesting.

There are big trucks and little taxis and
up and downtown buses with names and numbers.

Someone is always digging a hole in the pavement
with a pneumatic drill.
A building is being torn down.
Another is being built.
You can hear the blast of the dynamite.
You can see the trucks loading silt and rubble
and watch them unload concrete and cable and
plaster and plates of glass.

The policemen whistle. The cars whirr and rattle
as they change their gears to stop or go.

Sometimes a band marches by—a parade band or
a Salvation Army band with tambourines and a
big bass drum.

The whole city hums like a hive of bees.
It would be fun to spend all of your time
in the streets just looking and listening.

But children who live in the city must go to
school just like children everywhere.

You can walk to school if your school is close by.
If you are little, your father walks with you
on his way to work and your mother is waiting
for you when school is over.

Middle-sized children are sometimes picked up
by a school bus and taken home again after school.

Older children know how to get to school
and home again by themselves.

At a city school you learn the same things you
learn at any school, but at recess you go out to
play city games, either in the playground, or in the
street in front of your school, if the traffic has been
stopped and the street is blocked off so you have
a safe place to play.

There is not much space but there are lots of
things to do during recess.
You can play hopscotch.
You can skateboard and roller-skate.
You can play skipping games.
You can play ball.

It is so crowded it is hard not to throw a
ball through a school window. If this happens
you not only make someone angry but you
will probably lose your ball.

On Saturdays and Sundays and holidays
you can go to the park to play.
There is more space than on the streets
and different things to do.

There is a lake with swans and ducks to
feed, and rowboats in the spring.
In winter there is a long hill for
tobogganing and an ice-skating rink.

Weather isn't very important in a city.
Rain or shine, hot or cold,
you can go to the Zoo.
The Library is open.
You can go to a Museum,
to the Aquarium, the Planetarium
or to a theater to see a play.

You can go shopping.
There are big department stores with
UP and DOWN escalators
and things to buy on every floor—
toys or clothes, or pots and pans.
In a very big city
some shops are open
twenty-four hours a day,
three hundred and sixty-five days a year.

When you are hungry you can go out to eat
in a restaurant—any kind of restaurant—
an Indian restaurant, a Chinese restaurant
or a French café.
There are Kosher restaurants and Fish Bars
and Salad Bars and Health-food Cafeterias.

Would you like a pancake in a Pancake house?
Would you like a pizza in a Pizza parlor?
What about a nice hot cup of tea?

You can get any kind of food you want in a
city and nothing is ever out of season.
You can get strawberries in November
and asparagus in January.

You can buy a bagel from the bagel lady
or a bag of chestnuts from the chestnut man
on the streets of a big city in December.

Not everyone lives in a tall building
in the tallest part of the city.
In every city, especially if it is an old city,
there are neighborhoods that are almost
like small villages.

Here there are little leftover houses and
little leftover bakeries and butchers' shops
and fruit stands and flower stalls,
and people eat at home.

In an old neighborhood people know one another.
They greet each other on the street
and talk about the world and the football scores.
Some people even know your name.

There are curtains in the windows. There are
flowers in pots and boxes on the windowsills.
There might even be a small backyard
where you could keep a puppy.

Sometimes there are street parties or church
bazaars with banners and strings of lights
and balloons and games to play.
There are lotteries and shooting galleries
and fortune-tellers and food stands.

There is nothing that tastes as good as
a sizzling hot sausage with greasy green peppers
cooked at a street fair food stand.

When you go home to bed, you can still
see the lights and hear the sounds
from the neighboring street.

Even if your room
is on the top floor
of a big apartment house,
long after you are fast asleep
the lights of the city
will be shining on your ceiling.

A big city stays awake all night.
Neon signs blink on and off.
Traffic signals change from red to green.
Late buses stop or go.
Doormen whistle.
A taxi horn honks.

People are in the streets,
laughing and singing and shouting.

Far in the distance,
a siren answers a fire alarm.
A tugboat toots.
Underground, the trains rumble.

It is surprising how easy it is to sleep
through the sounds of a crowded city
if you are used to them.
But once in a while,
if you are wakeful,
you may imagine an underground railway
taking you out of the city to
a quiet place with lots of space.

A farm in the country is a quiet place with lots of space.
Your nearest neighbor's house may be a mile or more away. Though not so many people
live here, those who do will be good friends to you. Everyone will know your name.
And if there's no one about to talk to, there is always something worth looking at.

Beside your house there are barns and stables and toolsheds and tractorsheds.

There are fields and fences and streams and trees.

You can see an amazing amount of sky.

But a farm in the country is not quite as deserted and quiet as it seems.

Listen carefully.

Cows moo. Dogs bark. The sheep complain.

Cocks crow. Geese gabble. The cats meow. The tethered goat is bleating.

A combine whirrs and rattles.

A door slams. A shutter creaks. The wind gossips with the leaves.

You can feel the thunder in the distance.

You can hear the haybaler clank as the men hurry to bring in the hay before it rains.

Weather is important on a farm. Sometimes you need rain to make the seeds sprout.

Sometimes you need sun to make the crops grow. Sometimes it is too cold to go out

or too hot to stay in, but in any kind of weather there are things to do on a farm.

When the sky is gray and forbidding and the pond and streams are frozen, if the grour

To keep you warm, there is wood which can be brought in from the forest. With an early thaw there a

If it is stormy, you can play in the hayloft of the big barn where it is quiet and warm and dry. Or yo covered with snow, there are mile-long hills to slide down, ice-cold tracks to follow.

...es to fish and streams for boating. There is always an old farm dog who wants to play or walk with you.

...n find an out-of-the-way place to read a good book while the rain drums on the windowpanes.

On school days, rain or shine or hot or cold, all the children who live in the country must go to school, just like children everywhere.

The big children go to high school. The middle children go to the middle school. The little children go to the elementary school on the edge of the village.

If you live on a farm a long way out in the country, you must be driven to school or there may be a school bus to pick you up. If you live nearer the village you can bicycle to school. The children who live in the village walk to school by themselves.

At a village school you learn the same things you learn at a city school. You learn how to read and write and count. You may spend a little more time learning about farming and how to plant seeds out-of-doors instead of in window boxes, but you will also study art and music and history. You may make fewer museum trips and more hiking trips and at recess there is more than enough room to play. There is room for hide-and-seek and games of tag.

There is space for basketball and volleyball and baseball and football.

If you lose a ball over the fence, the only one who might mind will be a cow.

Some days your mother will pick you up after school if you have a dentist's appointment or you need new shoes. Then you have a chance to spend some time in the nearest small town. There is only one main street with shops but it has a clothes shop and a variety store and a bank. You can buy some candy or an ice cream or a book in the drug store.
You can buy nails and paint and tools and string in the hardware shop.
Most of the food shopping is done in a supermarket, where you can buy coffee and tea and sugar or flour and oatmeal, or vanilla and cocoa and raisins, which don't grow on the farm.

There are lots of things you do grow though, like pears and apples and all kinds of vegetables. You can buy vegetable seeds or seedlings from the nursery—lettuce and carrots and beans and radishes, onions and cabbages and tomatoes. Everything tastes so good when it is fresh from your garden. When you preserve your own vegetables in jars or in the deep-freeze, or make jam from your own strawberries, everything (with the possible exception of turnips) tastes especially good because it is yours.

Digging, raking, planting and weeding a garden is a lot of work, but it is worth it.

There is always work to be done on a farm. Older children help with the plowing and planting, the mowing, the haymaking and the harvest. Fences need mending. Wood must be cut and stacked. The middle children bring in the cows in the evening and put out the hay.
Even the little children help with the work on the farm.

You have to collect the eggs and feed and water the chickens.
Be sure they are *all* locked up at night or they won't *all* be there in the morning.
And all the farm work must be done before you even start your homework.
On a farm you are so tired at night you doze over your books after dinner.

Once you are in bed, you can scarcely stay awake long enough to say good night.
The lights are out early in the country.